This book belongs to:

_____

K. CO. KIDS Publishing
An imprint of K. CO. KIDS, LLC
5611 Colleyville Blvd., Suite 260, PMB #160, Colleyville, TX 76034

For more information regarding special discounts for bulk purchases, call K. CO. KIDS, LLC at (214) 693-5117 or e-mail us at info@kcokids.com.

This book was produced in conjunction with goodmedia communications, llc, Dallas, Texas.
www.goodmediacommunications.com

Cover illustration of Katie by Michael Albee.

Cover and interior design ©2008 TLC Graphics, www.TLCGraphics.com
Design by Monica Thomas

The text in this book is set in Shannon Book.

Manufactured in the United States of America
10 9 8 7 6 5 4 3 2 1

Library of Congress Cataloging-in-Publication Data

Kahanek, Kristine.
Katie And The Magic Umbrella: A Stormy Adventure / Kristine Kahanek
Illustrated by Michael Albee and Valerie Jimenez – 1st Edition
p. cm.
Library of Congress Control Number: 2008921055
Summary: During a storm, a guardian angel visits two children and teaches the children about rain, hail, thunder, lightning, and tornadoes. ◆ Audience ages 4–8
ISBN-13: 978-0-9801423-0-3
1. Storms—Juvenile fiction. 2. Guardian angels—Juvenile fiction.
[1. Storms—Fiction. 2. Weather—Fiction. 3. Guardian angels—Fiction.]
I. Albee, Michael, ill. II. Jimenez, Valerie, ill. III. Title.
PZ7.K12238Kat 2007   [E] QBI07-600303

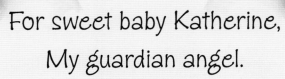

For sweet baby Katherine,

My guardian angel.

— and —

To Dad, who inspired my lifelong love of weather.

Illustrations by Michael Albee and Valerie Jimenez

Katie and the Magic Umbrella

A Stormy Adventure

by Kristine Kahanek

K. CO. KIDS Publishing ✦ Colleyville, Texas

Katie is a guardian angel. She wears a winged watch that glows and flutters when the children she protects need her. One night her special watch began to glow. She quickly grabbed her magic umbrella and flew from her home in Heaven to Earth down below.

Katie had to be careful. She could hear the rumble of thunder and see the flash of lightning off in the distance. She knew why Alex and Grace needed her. A thunderstorm was brewing.

Katie reached their bedroom window and peeped in. She could see Alex and Grace tucked in their beds with their faces barely peeking out from under their sheets. The storm was getting closer, and they were really getting scared.

Inside their bedroom, Grace suddenly felt something gently land on the edge of her bed. She looked, and there was Katie. With their mouths wide open, Grace and Alex looked at each other.

Then Grace asked, "Wow! Are you really an angel?"

Katie said, "You bet I am! I'm Katie, your guardian angel. I'm here to help you see that thunderstorms really aren't so scary."

Then Katie flew over to the window by Alex's bed. Looking outside she could see that the storm was getting stronger.

"I'm here to take you on a magical adventure! Once you understand how thunderstorms work, they won't be so scary anymore.

Of course, you should never go outside by yourself during a storm. But, tonight you're with me, and my magic umbrella will keep you safe!"

So, Alex and Grace took hold of the umbrella. In no time, they were flying high in the sky, watching the flashes of lightning from a distance.

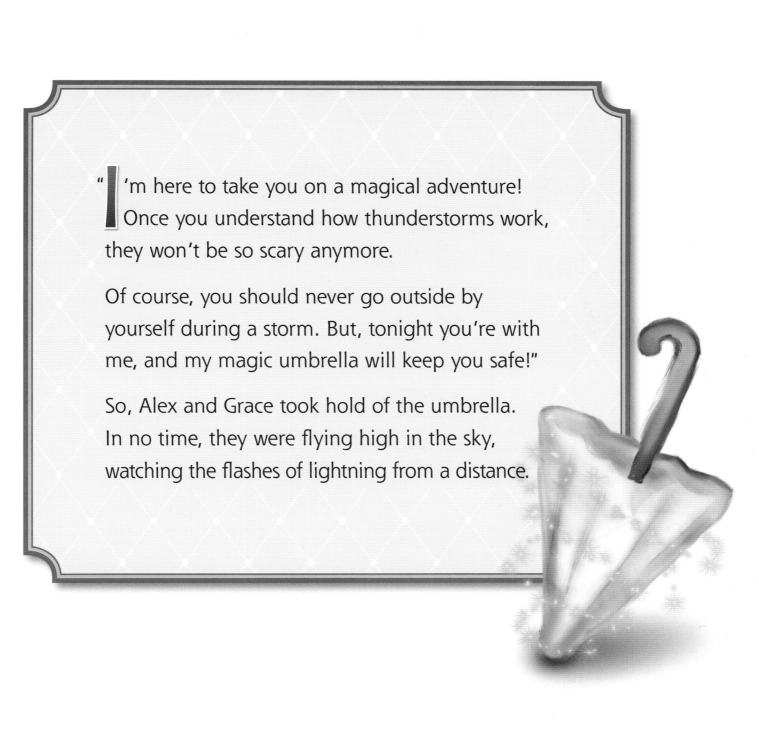

"This is one kind of cloud that can grow to make rain," Katie said as they all flew over to a fluffy white cloud.

"I've seen these before. They look like cotton balls!" exclaimed Grace.

"This is a cumulus cloud," Katie explained.

"A cumulo … what?" asked Alex.

Katie giggled. "Cumulus. It's a funny word, isn't it?"

Cumulus

"A cumulus cloud is made of tiny water drops that are so small you can't even see them. On warm, muggy days, these tiny drops are lifted by the sun's warmth high into the sky. Like magic, these cotton ball clouds grow bigger. Sometimes they grow into tall cumulus clouds that have so much water in them that the water spills over onto the earth, and that's how we get rain," explained Katie.

"I like cumulus clouds," Grace decided.

All of a sudden a big gust of wind came up and lifted Katie, Alex, and Grace up even higher in the sky. Katie pointed at the growing thunderstorm and said, "That is the other type of rain cloud—a cumulonimbus cloud."

"A cumulo … what?" asked Alex.

"Cumulonimbus," said Katie.

"Oooh … cu–mu–lo–nim–bus," the children said together.

"That's right," Katie said with a giggle. "The cumulonimbus cloud can be very frightening and dangerous. Along with rain, it also makes hail, tornadoes, lightning, and thunder."

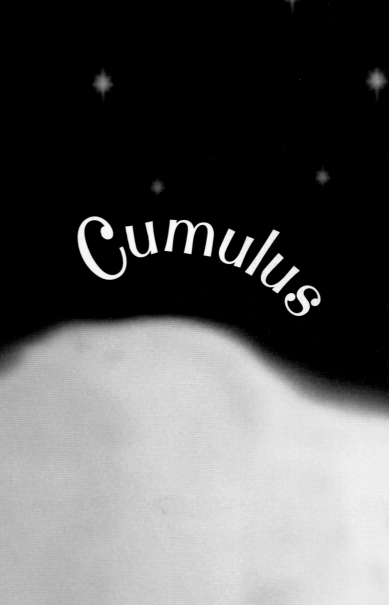

Cumulus

Cumulonimbus

Boom!

"Lightning is what causes thunder. Lightning is electricity and the flash is hotter than the surface of the sun! So hot, it makes the air crash together to make the loud sound of thunder. The closer you are to the lightning, the faster you hear the thunder."

"Watch the storm cloud closely," Katie told the children. "When you see a flash of lightning, count until you hear the thunder."

Grace and Alex watched until they saw a bolt. "1 … 2 … 3 … 4 … 5,"
KAA-BAM!

"Katie, I counted to five!" exclaimed Grace.

"That means the lightning flash is about one mile away." Katie explained that the more numbers you count between lightning and thunder, the farther you are from the worst of the storm.

ointing to another part of the storm, Alex exclaimed, "Grace, look over there! Those look like ice cubes flying in the air!"

"Those balls of ice are really called hailstones. When a storm is strong enough, these hailstones can form inside the highest part of the cloud. And, just like raindrops, they tumble to Earth when they become too heavy for the clouds to hold them. They can be as little as peas or as big as cantaloupes!"

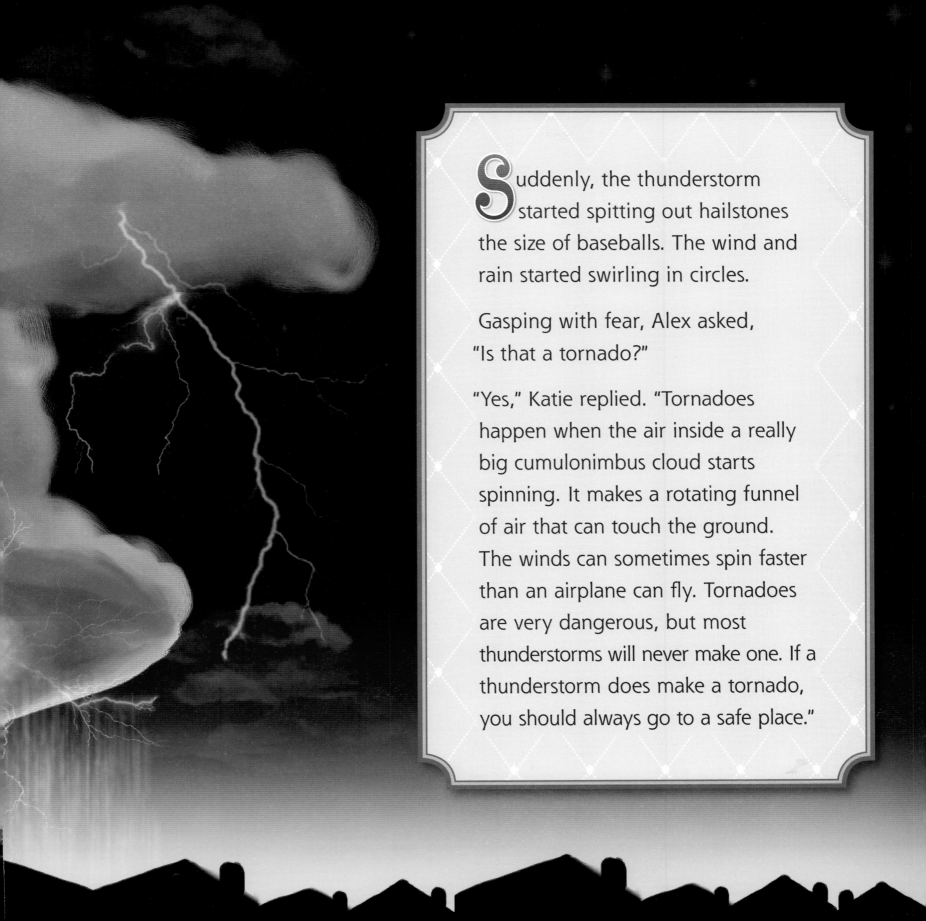

Suddenly, the thunderstorm started spitting out hailstones the size of baseballs. The wind and rain started swirling in circles.

Gasping with fear, Alex asked, "Is that a tornado?"

"Yes," Katie replied. "Tornadoes happen when the air inside a really big cumulonimbus cloud starts spinning. It makes a rotating funnel of air that can touch the ground. The winds can sometimes spin faster than an airplane can fly. Tornadoes are very dangerous, but most thunderstorms will never make one. If a thunderstorm does make a tornado, you should always go to a safe place."

It was time for their adventure to end. Katie pulled a secret pouch from her pocket, and with a flick of her finger she released sparkling angel dust that swirled like magic all around the dark, menacing twister. The tornado began to glow in all colors of the rainbow as it disappeared back into the cloud.

The next thing they knew, Alex and Grace were back in their room, but not in bed. Instead, they were in the closet.

Peeking through her dresses, Grace asked, "What are we doing in here? I know! This is our safe place."

"That's right Grace. This is where you should stay until the storm passes," Katie explained.

"Can you wait with us Katie?" Grace asked.

Katie hugged the children and said, "It's time for me to go back to my home in Heaven. Always remember, I am just a wish away. Anytime you need me, my special watch will let me know."

When the storm blew over, the children stepped out of the closet to find moonlight shining through their window. With a yawn and a stretch, they crawled back in bed and immediately fell into a peaceful sleep.

Grace and Alex woke up to a beautiful spring morning and wondered if their stormy adventure had been just a dream.

Alex pointed to the corner of their room. "Grace, look!"

Right there in the corner was Katie's magic umbrella, ready for Grace and Alex's next adventure with their guardian angel.

Let's Talk About It!

1. Why do you think Alex and Grace were frightened by the thunderstorm?

2. Is there really such a thing as a magic umbrella?

3. Can your umbrella keep you safe outside during a thunderstorm?

4. Is it safe to be outside at all during a thunderstorm?

5. Do you remember which cloud is the thunderstorm? What types of weather does it make?

Let's Talk About It!

6. What causes thunder? And what does it sound like?

7. How do lightning and thunder help you to know how far away the storm is?

8. What is hail? Have you ever seen it before?

9. How do tornadoes form?

10. Does every thunderstorm make a tornado?

11. Where is the safest place to be inside your home during a thunderstorm?

Answers on the next page.

Answers to
Let's Talk About It!

1. Children discuss their thoughts.

2. No.

3. No. Umbrellas can only keep you dry in a rain shower. They are not safe to use if there is thunder and lightning.

4. No.

5. Cumulonimbus: rain, lightning, thunder, hail, wind, and tornadoes

6. Thunder is the sound caused by the hot flash from a lightning bolt. It makes a loud clapping or booming sound.

7. The amount of time between a lightning strike and the sound of thunder determines how far away the storm is. Every five seconds equals one mile.

Answers to
Let's Talk About It!

8. Balls of ice that form during a thunderstorm.

9. Tornadoes can form when air inside a really big cumulonimbus cloud starts spinning. It makes a rotating funnel of air that can touch the ground. The winds inside this funnel can spin fast enough to do damage and are very dangerous.

10. No. Most thunderstorms never create a tornado.

11. The safest place to be during a thunderstorm is underground in a storm cellar or basement. If you do not have a basement, the safest place to be is in a first floor room with no windows, such as a bathroom, pantry, closet, or storage room.

Weather Words

Atmosphere

The atmosphere is the layer of gases that surround a planet. Earth's atmosphere is divided into five layers: exosphere, thermosphere, mesosphere, stratosphere, and troposphere.

Cirrus

Cirrus clouds are thin, wispy clouds that form high in the atmosphere. These clouds are made of ice crystals.

Clouds

Clouds are formed by the collection of tiny water droplets or, at colder temperatures, ice crystals floating in the air above the surface. Clouds come in many different sizes and shapes. When clouds form at ground level, they are called fog. Clouds can form high in the atmosphere and everywhere in between. Clouds provide information that help us to understand the weather.

Cumulus

Cumulus clouds are fluffy, mid-level clouds that often look like cotton balls. These clouds usually indicate fair weather, but if they grow high enough in the atmosphere, they can eventually make rain.

Cumulonimbus

Cumulonimbus clouds are otherwise called thunderstorms. They normally make lightning, thunder, gusty winds, and rain. These are vertical clouds that can grow more than 10 miles high in the atmosphere. Some cumulonimbus clouds become so strong they can make hail and even tornadoes.

Earth

Earth is the planet we live on. It is the third planet from the sun.

Funnel Cloud

A funnel cloud is a spinning column of air that extends downward from the bottom of a very strong thunderstorm. If the funnel cloud reaches the ground, then it is called a tornado.

Hail

Hail or hailstones, are balls of ice that form high inside a very strong thunderstorm. Hailstones are made of layers of ice. 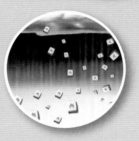 They grow as powerful gusts of wind move them up and down inside the cloud, causing them to collide with raindrops. These drops stick and refreeze on the hailstone, adding more layers until it gets so heavy it falls to Earth.

Lightning

Lightning is a bright flash of light caused by a discharge of static electricity during a thunderstorm. A single  lightning bolt can heat the air to more than 54,000° Fahrenheit. That is hotter than the surface of the sun! Lightning can strike three different ways: cloud to cloud, cloud to air, and cloud to ground. Cloud to ground is the most dangerous to people.

Precipitation

Precipitation is a general name for water in any form falling from clouds. This includes rain, drizzle, hail, snow, and sleet.

Rain

Water droplets that fall from a cloud are called rain.

Rainbow

Rainbows are shaped like an arc. They are multi-colored with red on the outside and purple on the inside. Rainbows  form in the sky when the sun shines onto raindrops as they fall from the clouds.

Stratus

Stratus clouds are low-level clouds that are usually dark and gray. These clouds normally don't bring rain but can sometimes produce light rain, light snow, or drizzle.

Sun

The sun is 93 million miles away from the earth but is responsible for most of our weather. The sun's heat provides energy to the earth's atmosphere. The sun is a star that is 868,000 miles wide and exists in the center of our solar system.

Weather Words

Sunrise
Sunrise is the time of day the sun begins to rise above the eastern horizon.

Sunset
Sunset is the time of day the sun begins to fall below the western horizon.

Thunder
Thunder is the booming sound that occurs when the air surrounding a bolt of lightning expands and contracts.

Thunderstorm
A thunderstorm is produced by a cumulonimbus cloud and always has lightning and thunder. Most thunderstorms contain rain and gusty winds, and if they are strong enough, they can produce large hail and even tornadoes.

Tornado
A tornado is a violently rotating column of air that drops down from the bottom of a very strong thunderstorm. A tornado is usually first visible as a funnel cloud. Once the funnel reaches the ground it is called a tornado. Tornadoes can be as little as a few hundred feet wide to more than a mile wide and can travel at speeds of 25–55 mph. Winds inside a tornado range from as little as 40 mph to more than 300 mph. The damage caused by tornadoes is measured by the Enhanced Fujita Scale or EF-Scale.

Weather
Weather is the condition of the atmosphere at a particular time and place.

Wind
Wind is the movement of air relative to the surface of the earth.

An acclaimed television meteorologist who has been forecasting weather in Texas for nearly 20 years, Kristine Kahanek received her Bachelor of Science in Meteorology from Texas A&M University. She is certified by both the American Meteorological Society and the National Weather Association. Kristine lives with her husband and two children in a suburb of Dallas/Ft. Worth.

For ordering information and more
fun with Katie, Grace, and Alex, please visit
www.KatieandtheMagicUmbrella.com.